AI FOR EVERYONE

AI FOR EVERYONE

Understanding and Harnessing Artificial Intelligence

GIDEON RAYBURN

publisher logo
Revival Waves of Glory Books & Publishing

CONTENTS

1	Introduction to Artificial Intelligence	1
2	Ethical and Social Implications of AI	5
3	Key Concepts in AI	11
4	Applications of AI	15
5	Building AI Solutions	19
6	Future Trends in AI	23

Copyright © 2024 by Gideon Rayburn
All rights reserved. No part of this book may be reproduced in any manner whatsoever without written permission except in the case of brief quotations embodied in critical articles and reviews.
First Printing, 2024

CHAPTER 1

Introduction to Artificial Intelligence

Welcome to the field of AI! If you have picked up this book because you are interested in learning about AI, you are making a good choice. As someone who has worked in the field for a long while, I am very excited about the impact AI is having on the world. This is a powerful, transformative technology that will affect how business, government, education, healthcare, and a host of other fields affect their bottom line. A solid understanding of AI will be important if you are in business, if you manage people, if you are involved in politics or any government-related activity, if you are in the service industry, if you are a student, or if you are a member of the general population that wants to work or live in a country with an edge.

The AI community has been very good about educating peers about important techniques and developments, as any field should be. But a niche is a niche, and our field has sometimes been less good at talking to outsiders about what AI is, what it does, what it can do, and, importantly, what to expect with regard to its impact. This book is an attempt to remedy that situation. It is not a technical book aimed at practitioners, nor is it a long list of specific ways AI is, or will be, affecting our daily lives, though I discuss quite a few examples. Rather, it provides a general overview of the key ideas and techniques of AI and it outlines a number of challenges we face while inventing the field. The focus is on a broad understanding of the field, which means I talk about the "what" and "why" of AI, but not the "how" - other texts, of which there are many, do that already. The title of the book is "AI for Everyone: Building Knowledge and an AI literate establishment."

Definition and Scope of AI

Usually, we do not take results that follow so quickly and directly from definitions to be interesting. But in this case, I think it is worth pausing just a little to think about what these definitive relationships imply. The first thing is that if we try to define human intelligence in this way, we get the surprising conclusion that human intelligence does not involve thought. Surely, that is an unexpected move. More carefully speaking, this definition of AI takes us into the realm of decisions that are really quite easy and quick for human beings. Married to the statistical ideas of machine learning that we will introduce later, it is remarkably powerful the processes that carry out thought in this sense really do work on quite a lot of problems that we find difficult. In fact, there is a theory of intelligence that derives human intelligence as one possible implementation of this general set of algorithms.

The field of artificial intelligence, or AI, goes back to the very beginnings of computer science. And, in its original and in some ways still the most widely understood meaning, is the creation of programs that perform tasks that would otherwise require human intelligence. The tasks are generally, but not always, ones that people are better at. And, as we will see, the criterion need not be that the program does better (i.e., more accurately or more quickly), just that it might be judged to be using its head - as opposed to being, say a fast computer-controlled response to the environment in which it finds itself. However, as we will also see, the meaning of the subject has been much broadened.

Brief History of AI

Today, some six decades after A. M. Turing's monumental paper on what is now known as the Turing test, Artificial Intelligence has undergone a profound shift as a field. To explain this shift, we start by providing a brief history of the field. The formative years of AI innovation owe a great deal to the work of Turing, Jacques von Neumann, Marvin Minsky, and others. Three ideas were embraced: intelligence can be thought of as a mechanical process; it is possible to describe that process exactly through a series of mathematical steps; and any intelligent process could conceptually be performed by a machine. This way, these early AI pioneers were laying the foundations for a fully connected global society, anticipating a shared intelligence infrastructure.

On a fall night in Santa Barbara, California, in 1985, a young journalist named John Markoff was joining Patrick Winston, a computer scientist and member of the faculty of the Massachusetts Institute of Technology AI Laboratory, for dinner. Over fish and wine in a small town near the Stanford Linear Accelerator, Winston explained to Markoff how researchers were trying to build systems that could perform as well as, or better than, humans in certain problem-solving tasks. "We're going to make machines smart," he said, emphasizing the word "smart." In the same year, the Nobel laureate Herbert A. Simon, a pioneer in AI, encapsulated the objectives of the field as follows: "A computer does something that, if done by a person, would be said to involve intelligence... These achievements are remarkable. They have captured the allegiance and the imagination of a generation of computer scientists around the world."

Types of AI Systems

The systems that think like human capability involves the cognitive ability of a machine to replicate human thoughts, i.e., human thinking. It constitutes understanding its environment, interacting with the environment effectively, and drawing inferences from the data collected during interaction. These systems are given these capabilities so that they are able to think and act like humans. One subpart of the systems that think like human AI capabilities is that of natural language processing (NLP). This constituent of AI deals with the coding of human languages, therefore providing it with the authority to comprehend as well as communicate. It involves the complete understanding of the rules as well as word structures, both semantic and grammatical. NLP aims at enabling human understanding using machines. The very first major constraint of NLP was spelling, and since then NLP has come a long way. It has developed such that it has capacities to support spell checks as well as predictive text texting in the day-to-day life of a person.

AI was categorized into four different types in the most widely accepted method of classification. The four different types of AI systems are systems that think like humans, systems that act like humans, systems that think rationally, and systems that act rationally. According to this classification, machines that act or think like humans have to possess characteristics that are found in a human.

CHAPTER 2

Ethical and Social Implications of AI

In this situation, AI systems are only human to a limited extent, only as fair as their human designers, and only as safe or useful as their human users. Therefore, there is a need to develop AI systems whose purpose is to serve society by making reliable and safe AI systems with both short- and long-term benefits. Like other technologies, AI is not inherently good or bad, although some uses may be more ethical than others. As we become a more mature and technologically advanced species, we must begin to take responsibility for the very intelligent machines that are beginning to emerge. I envision an AI that comes out in the open from specialized technical solutions and opaque systems to become a technology open to understanding, to discussions, and to criticism, a new form of collective intelligence that can help us solve problems that are beyond the broadest intense human-based computational capabilities. This will require the active collaboration of researchers in different technical fields such as regulation, ethics, and social sciences, as well as industry, the public and private sector, and large collaborative public initiatives.

All new technologies also raise questions about the appropriate uses of those technologies. The same will be true for the intelligent machines we may soon be creating. AI, in mimicking human intelligence and automating decision making, often operates autonomously. The use of AI raises unique ethical questions. Although there may be guidelines and regulations for AI developers or users, the ability to violate them is usually more significant than with previous technologies. Assigning responsibility for AI decisions to programmers, hardware managers, data providers, or users may not always be acceptable. For many AI decisions, it is not clear who or what to hold accountable. Moreover, many aspects of AI design, particularly as the technology has become more complex, means the development, evaluation, and validation of AI is not nearly as transparent as the design of many forms of traditional software.

Privacy and Security Concerns

AI is a data-driven technology, and the advancement in recent years is largely due to many large-scale successes in the use of data for building machine-learned models. These models rely on such data not only being available but also being in good supply, at low cost, and in configurations or structures that lend to their being used effectively. As data rates increase, the amount of personal, business, and civic data being stored, processed, and shared follow in kind. Consequently, one of the most persistent questions that must be asked is what data should and should not be in the public domain. It is an important concern, especially as the sensors and devices of modern life, from environmental monitors to fitness bands to home assistants, collect and send more data to private sector and federal data stores. Efforts to address data privacy range from careful reviews of data linking across public records and premium digital content, to regulatory prohibitions on Wi-Fi sniffing and unauthorized data collection, to policy statements that square surveillance and privacy protections with open research and data discovery.

Recent advancements in AI have led to the careful analysis of various societal and ethical implications. In assessing these consequences of the rapid adoption of AI technologies in technical, managerial, and policymaking contexts, perhaps the most persistent and important concern lies along the lines of privacy and security. The increased availability of data from personal, business, and civic life necessitates a parallel increase in the understanding of the potential misuse, abuse, and protection of such data. This chapter reviews some of the societal, economic, and ethical pressures that drive privacy and security concerns and addresses some of the research efforts that seek to improve decision making, mitigation, and policy.

Bias and Fairness in AI

A consensus has been reached that fairness is a perceived and real human value concern, and that systems that do not exhibit the desired fair behaviour are judged to be failing. The data-flows, analysis, and self-improvement loops implicit in AI make it essential that sources of bias in contributing platforms (like data processing algorithms and AI models), as well as many work and decision-making systems in which they are employed, are identified. The concept of fairness is human-centric and defines the desire for impartial and tailored treatment. Different fairness definitions are currently used across different disciplines, and even within the same discipline, contradicting each other. These unfair AI models have their ethical values compromised. Also, fairness-aware AI is currently facing the challenges related, but not limited, to the development of systems that respond to explicitly provided fairness criteria, simultaneously and virtually proportional; detecting multiple forms of bias in the data and remedying them; and tracing and isolating sources of unfairness.

An algorithm - hard coded to differentiate between white and black faces - wrongfully deciphers the happiness of white people as the expression of most happiness, and the fury in black people as the maximum expression of anger. An entity that uses AI to process job applications ends up preferring men over women. A commercially used predictive policing system is steered towards sending more police officers to black neighbourhoods. A set of people-generated video clips endorsing political candidates wrongly identifies the candidates as running for political office and being in violation of election issues. A system for assessing resumes is favouring resumes coming from faux ethnic groups like Men, Only, and Yao, a fabricated group that is not actually represented.

Impact on Employment

There are a wide variety of simple manual jobs that the currently most advanced AI can do very accurately and quickly. A second observation is that machines can be developed to perform these tasks much cheaper than the humans who currently do them. As AI improves, it will make an increasing number of more cognitively demanding white-collar professional, marketing, and technical expert jobs redundant or economically unviable. In addition, longer lives, by increasing the efficiency of producing goods and services, AI provides an effective and direct way of improving living standards. AI has already made many contributions to ensuring our current longer lives are spent in good health by increasing the efficiency of providing health services. In the narrow sense, AI also contributes directly to the efficiency of healthcare by automating and personalizing medical diagnostics and treatments. In the wider sense, AI can also improve living standards by, for example, providing transportation and increasing human safety or utility.

The ultimate aim for most firms is to make a profit for their shareholders by selling their products or services at the highest price relative to the costs of production. However, to make a profit requires that someone can and will buy their product. In the long run, an organization can only afford to pay wages to workers that are less than the added value of what they can produce. If workers can produce less value than the machines provided, the owners of the machines can then appropriate this difference as profit. In other words, in the long term, wages are proportional to how much value added workers provide.

CHAPTER 3

Key Concepts in AI

The following simple concepts are helpful in understanding what AI can and cannot do, and identifying possible uses of AI.

AI is simply a computer software that is able to learn and solve problems based on analysis of the data it processes. It does this by finding and exploiting patterns in data. For instance, AI can recognize a face, understand a spoken voice or written language, understand the content of an image, drive a car autonomously, navigate a warehouse or a retail store, optimize materials and production processes, recommend products one is likely to appreciate, and perform many other activities that would require some level of human intelligence. AI creates value for its users by automating complex, bespoke, and less predictable cognitive tasks where humans have traditionally been the solution.

AI has limitations. It cannot invent a new goal, it cannot form its own understanding of the world or decide what things are of interest to it, and it cannot operate beyond the data and processing it is provided. AI solves problems as trained to do, automatically and continuously, from input in the form of data, settings or objectives, interactive input, and other constraints. AI generalizes well at a relevant scale, is robust to interference, and consistently produces outcomes that make sense. Therefore, dealing with AI should involve managing its impacts, including those relating to job displacement, ethical use, and disparities in access.

Machine Learning

We might be given a dataset that contains details of the individuals, with features such as age, education, hours of work per week, and so on. We could also be given the income of individuals in the dataset. With this data in hand, the learning algorithm could learn a mapping between the input and output, that is, a function that can be used to predict the desired output for any other age, with the degree of accuracy defined by the labels in the supplied dataset.

Machine learning consists of types of learning. In supervised learning, the algorithm is given labeled data. That is, the desired output for each input is provided. The learning algorithm provides us with a general rule that maps inputs to outputs. Consider an example where we want to build a model to predict yearly earnings of people in a certain country.

Machine learning is one of the fastest growing areas of computer science, with far-reaching applications. The aim of this chapter is to provide a concise overview of machine learning, explaining all the major concepts. At the end of the chapter, we provide some tips on how to prepare data for our algorithms; this is important because in practice a considerable portion of a researcher's or practitioner's time can be spent on this.

Deep Learning

While imitating the structure of the human brain, deep learning trains computers to perform human-like tasks, such as recognizing speech, identifying images, and making predictions. With the help of deep learning, we are now able to solve a greater number of problems than ever before. It is thought that the growth in the availability of data and the improvement in computer hardware has also accelerated the growth of deep learning and artificial intelligence. In a machine learning model, learning means getting better at a task, and hence, the training data should enable learning. Most deep learning uses supervised learning, a learning paradigm requiring large amounts of data. We can capture the input/output mapping by feeding a variety of labeled training examples into a model, enabling the model to make predictions. The 3 key components required for deep learning are: a model, objective, and training data.

Neural Networks
Or solving for facial recognition. Photos of faces are essentially a combination of pixels. Each pixel is a characteristic of the face such as the distance between eyes or color of the hair. The task is to estimate certain characteristics using the features which are pixels. This is a delicate process, since photos and pixels, taken apart, look nothing like a cat. And the crucial thing is we, who build computer models, don't know what an image is, at least not in the same way the model "knows" it – we don't know the criteria which the model uses for making decisions about the input.

Behind the machine learning news is a class of algorithms called a neural network. A neural network is a series of algorithms that strives to recognize underlying relationships in a set of data through a process that mimics the way the human brain operates. Neural networks can adapt to complex, non-linear relationships in the data. We'll be talking a lot about what exactly that means, so let's begin with a primer. Suppose that you are trying to decide if a photo contains a cat or not. You first tell the computer the features – the eyes, the tail, the body and so on – and then the computer, using its superior processing power, goes through millions of photos, figures out the patterns that make an image a cat image, and tells you the ones that are a cat.

CHAPTER 4

Applications of AI

Some obvious benefits come by using AI for various medical and emergency tasks. For example, in the case of heart attacks and strokes, the critical first hour after symptoms begin is the golden opportunity to significantly increase the chance of survival and recovery. Currently, 80 percent of brain damage occurs in the golden hour. Even 15 minutes can make a significant difference. But, if symptoms are mild, they may still not be recognized until minutes later! Since a delayed reaction could be too late, existing smartwatch and phone technologies are already working to use AI algorithms to detect subtle signs before a disaster strikes, and take appropriate actions! These may soon join current technologies that don't require specific body sensors, as these methods rely on voice data and smart homes instead. These technologies have also spread to other domains. For example, in airports, we are able to use AI to predict maintenance and flight delays, manage security checks and baggage, etc. In agriculture areas, there are capabilities for precision agriculture and drone detection, etc.

    A wide variety of AI technologies are making our lives easier, whether we realize it or not. Some use everyday words, but operate behind the scenes, such as taking a picture with your smartphone and getting an automatic response about who is in it. Others use specific vocabulary that is too intimidating for us to give a second thought, like using "natural language processing" in a medical interface to understand!

Healthcare

What is considered to be very good care by one patient can be not good for another one. Which patient's interest at the moment should the AI protect? What about patients with a chronic disease who would prefer to die rather than to live through constant pain day and night? Which moral principles should be applied? AI could generate some improvements in the provision of healthcare.

Over the last decades, AI has been used to diagnose patients, plan treatments, and arrange schedules of treatments in many diseases. Of course, AI can only take care of certain aspects of healthcare, but it can create new ideas and values of work for managers of care. With the new generation of medical instruments, AI manages to carry out vascular surgery or replacement of knee and hip joints as well. This way, such complicated surgeries become more accurate. There is no role of a doctor in the process, who would be tired and his attention would be reduced. Nevertheless, we will not get around all the problems connected with care. Neither all the diseases are still cured, nor are the patients always happy.

Finance

Finance is one of the hottest fields in AI research, with the world's best headhunted by companies like Google and Facebook. In high-frequency stock trading, in mathematical terms, even one microsecond is a unit of time that is much too long. Hence, today's main task for stock traders is to reduce computer access, wait time, and data processing methods so as to trade in the most advanced or the most competitive way using computer programs. According to the Tabb Group, the global financial service securities processing cost assessment reached US$14 billion in 2008, and this figure is expected to grow. On August 8, 2011, United States Standard & Poor's downgraded the long-term investment credit ratings of the Federation of the United States. On August 15, 2011, the FTSE China A50 futures consumption ratio exceeded 2.4, contracting for 210,943 contracts. Since Standard & Poor's downgraded the long-term investment credit rating of the Federation of the United States, the FTSE China A50 index has plummeted by a rank of over 10%, and ultra-short-term speculators entered the market intensively within 6 days (average statistical interest at the time of the peak hour). The Federation of American Securities Corporation (CFTC) suspiciously checked or fined HKIRA.

Transportation

Logistics: Logistics companies use AI in a wide variety of capacities. The problem of routing vehicles was previously mentioned in this section in the context of ride-sharing. Logistics companies also have problems of scheduling and routing other resources, such as time and labor. Services provided by these companies are subject to large seasonal variability, and the forecast of demand for time or labor is an important problem. Decisions about how much inventory to carry are addressed by forecasting demand for specific products. Customer service can also be improved using data and AI techniques. Many companies which use fixed pricing mechanisms could benefit from data-driven dynamic pricing methods.

Ride-sharing: Ride-sharing companies are currently developing AI technology in a number of directions. A few companies are developing self-driving technology in the hope that it can be used to reduce driver costs. Another popular area of AI research in ride-sharing is route optimization, both in terms of matching users to vehicles and in terms of routing vehicles. These companies also develop AI technology to analyze user behavior and preferences. With large amounts of data on what users desire relative to their choices, it is possible to solve difficult problems in demand estimation. This technology is used to determine how many drivers to have and where.

Self-driving vehicles: Self-driving cars have recently become a popular technology due to breakthroughs in artificial intelligence, and it will probably become more common in the coming years. The potential impact of this technology on the average person is large, due to the pervasiveness of the automobile's role in everyday life. A nontrivial number of Americans spend over an hour a day driving, and self-driving cars will allow them to spend this time more productively. Self-driving car technology is at the intersection of several fields including computer vision, robotics, planning, controls, and mechanical engineering. AI is used to create the decision-making components of self-driving car systems.

CHAPTER 5

Building AI Solutions

There are several steps that you must go through when you build AI. These steps are: first, you have to know it, and then you have to state your design correctly. Then you choose your AI algorithm. After this, you measure its performance, and with these measurements, you refine the design according to the measured results. You build the learning AI system and put it into operation with the steps. Artificial intelligence isn't magic. When building AI systems, it's essential to obey these steps. The first step is to determine the problem. Then, define your design. The next step is to design your learning AI system. Then you put your learning AI system into operation. After putting AI into operation, you have to maintain it.

We know what AI is capable of and we are aware of how we can use AI. Now the question is, "How can we build AI solutions?" Here are a few steps to guide you in building AI solutions. First and foremost, you should know what the problem is, and then you have to design the solution in a good way. Using this knowledge in AI, you can build an algorithm. Once you have built the AI solution with the first step, you should measure it, and after taking these measurements, you can refine the harmonization according to the measured results. Next, you need to build the system and put it into operation. AI isn't magic; we cannot build an AI system with vague goals.

Solutions to problems will be different when they are put into precise questions. When building AI, the design is very important. You have to choose the most suitable solution to the question. You have to measure it, tune it, operate it, and maintain it.

Data Collection and Preprocessing

For the next-level pilots, the team must have considerable expertise in collecting and integrating the data and will need this expertise in place when the pilot is approved to ensure that data needs can be met in a timely fashion. This team will initially work with data from a variety of sources and is generally associated with proper governance, security, and compliance that may be independent of line of business groups. While this step necessitates a new set of data abilities, the data and systems used still scale with no performance needs exceeding the existing levels. The use of exploratory data analysis is a key step in the iterative process of data exploration.

After identifying the data needs, companies must focus on acquiring the data needed for AI. While organizations increasingly gather and store large amounts of data, relevant data may still be hard to come by due to privacy and regulatory concerns or due to data being scattered across different parts of the company. For these initial incubation stage projects, the data used can be small in size, and data obtained from existing data warehousing systems can generally be utilized. Also, the data-related tasks are small, teams are close, or no integration is required with other teams, and training data is obtained from adjacent systems and databases. Such a level of effort, plus adequate connectivity, can be done via the line of business groups.

Model Selection and Training

When you have chosen which model to use, the next task is to find the right algorithm to train the model. Techniques associated with training are often referred to as the learning algorithm. This step, learning, involves running an algorithm that will scan and memorize the rows of data and discover the functional relationships between features and labels.

Once feature representation is done, choosing the right model involves choosing what you might call the model architecture. Beginning with choosing the right model architecture is called model selection. For most predictions that depend on ordered data, such as time series sales predictions or predictions of not purchased, preferred promoted product, purchased product, learning to rank models, that can take into account user context etc., different types of neural networks are most commonly used as a model. Making the right choice here entails not just picking a neural network, but selecting the right variant of the neural network, or creating a new type of neural network that is appropriate for your specific business problem.

Evaluation and Deployment

After a machine learning model has been trained, it can then be deployed (make the model available to applications) to serve a particular function. Deployment of the model could be as simple as plugging it into an application or exposing its predictions as a service. It often requires managing a resource-intensive distributed service such as world-class, high-throughput, load-balanced backend services and requires monitoring tools and mechanisms. More complex deployments may also need tools and mechanisms that can help to evaluate the extent to which the models are performing their task and also to debug any identified performance problems.

Evaluate the model and ensure that the results of the model are as expected. Unpredicted or unexpected results could potentially affect a wide range of users. Be careful about biases resulting from limitations and underlying information. Evaluate the model on unseen data and also in the context of how the system would be used in practice. Modify the data, the model, and the problem to make machine learning models that are more robust in the field. It can often be challenging to interpret model decisions. We should build methods that can help users interpret model outputs.

CHAPTER 6

Future Trends in AI

For only in the past several years have we learned to effectively train computers to recognize objects, understand speech or language, convert languages, play complicated games or recommend interesting movies to watch. The most effective AI applications involve multiple AI capabilities coordinated to create new interactive, data services and solutions possible. Consequently, we are just at the beginning of a trend that promises to change every field of human activity in significant ways. We are approaching the golden age of AI. AI truly has the potential to help humanity address some of its most serious challenges. AI generates revenues for companies that employ a retail strategy, leverage data resources that have a possibility of significant leverage, maintain closed access in clouds, and grow by attracting interest from a broad range of applications. The most powerful and successful AI companies in the world were well tuned to the value proposition of a large AI system: providing valuable data services to a massive number of people. These large-scale, online businesses are foundational companies. Their services are integrated into the fabric of large economies.

This chapter explores six trends that are likely to have a significant impact on the future of AI. They include increasing data, the ascendance of machine learning, the growth of independent AI disciplines, the importance of context, the rapid increase in software efficiency, and the global diffusion of AI potential. Quite a few critical factors will shape how these trends play themselves out over the next several years. They include economic, scientific, societal, and political considerations. The race to make the most effective use of increasingly large AI systems will likely involve a number of unexpected developments. While many powerful organizations will be the most effective in absorbing these new technologies to serve their own needs, the large level of diffusion argues that a large number of people will use AI to better serve humanity everywhere. The results should be astounding.

Explainable AI

To summarize quite a bit of literature, most progress in this direction is available in the domain of image recognition. The image had to typically undergo an existence of server filtering smooth or average 7 incorrectly classified coke. Visualizing model features were a bit easier using techniques such as deconvolution and saliency maps to a ReLU-based model. Saliency or Hidden Feature attribution could trace data points to those neurons that it triggers if data is slightly altered. The key approach is to plot pre-screen or decode the inputs that are mapped to a set of feature neurons that must be present for activation of a particular neuron or a particular class in panel e. That is, if the blocks or the features had a high saliency with respect to the neuron or the class label for the model, then they must have played an important role in the outcome of the network meta classifier that it was supposed to explain their outputs off.

To improve the model performance, what was needed were the goodness and the evils. And goodness and the evils in the deep learning model and in models in AI in general were, if anything, less understood than literature climate change. The proposed avenue out of this confusion was a method called Explainable AI or XAI. The idea was to directly visualize and explain the behavior of the algorithm, applying the latest tools and technologies to directly visualize the inputs and outputs of the deep net. Nando de Freitas was the father of this field. However, there were two major sets of limitations also to this approach. One, Bayesian probability densities outputs that we wanted to get out of the model also are hard to construct in high-dimensional space that was needed for the problem. Kodak and Greg Hinton hosted a 2013 summer school on this topic.

So far, we discussed the concepts of models and the training of models. We found that the entire essence of AI depended on good training. And all the lessons in this book are essentially on how to get the best training. The key element of training, apart from the data, features, and the model, were the objective functions. The objective functions determined the effectiveness of the model. The loss function was the measure of this objective function. The goal of training was to minimize the loss functions. This need for minimization of loss functions was one of the main reasons for the success of deep learning non-linear models. These could finally get trained with much less human intervention compared to the traditional linear models. If the models were really deep and had got trained better than humans, then it was expected that they performed better on the loss function. However, much to the surprise and dismay of the human workers in the model, there were numerous examples such as the one below where the model and the human disagreed.

AI Ethics and Regulation

The bottom line is that Technology Ethics does not thrive in a void; it needs to engage with the real-world problems and challenges of technological development. When the ethical concerns and issues are not addressed or ignored by a company or a society, that company or society risks a backlash from customers, users, and citizens which, in many cases, are justified and whose recurrence would hinder or destroy innovation. As such, it is evident that the tech world needs a set of rules that serve the goodwill of all stakeholders. This text tries to shine light on some of these fundamental rules in AI.

The primary goal of these groups is to anticipate what might go wrong and how poverty, unemployment, the digital divide, inequality, privacy violations, negative biases, power abuses, security risks, and detrimental unfair labor practices could be addressed by legislation, corporate policies, codes of ethics, international agreements, commissions, and other measures that address ethical values, obligations, and perils of the digital age.

However, they seem to be left alone, forced to make tough judgment calls on every desirable and fledgling technological application, in settings that are almost exclusively dominated by the government and the global corporation, the bank and the monopoly. The pressure to shift our aim from good to greed is simply too high. Even the powerful corporations themselves are aware of this imbalance. They formed consulting groups and sought help and advice from various international bodies, including the UN, who showed interest in a process that would require participation from all stakeholders: designers, developers, investors, users, experts, and consumers.

Regrettably, virtually all technological innovations have the potential to be misused, corrupted, abused, hacked, or misinterpreted - our experience teaches us that the race for bigger profits greatly exceeds the concerns for what might go wrong. Such concerns have led to a cry for help from many thoughtful pioneers and leaders of the software and hardware industry, as well as from the majority of the people who are fascinated, puzzled, thrilled, and excited by the continuing revolution in bioinformatics, big data and social media analytics, machine learning, robotics, and artificial intelligence, and who would consecrate their talents and careers to foster growth and keep innovation alive.

Our politicians, who represent us, have the power to regulate, or if necessary, prohibit particular technologies, in order to protect public interest and common values. However, very often the politicians are not informed or experienced enough to govern technology; nor are they sufficiently enlightened to perform well in the complex, rapidly-changing, and cutthroat world of technology, where everyone's hands are constantly being forced.

The general public expects that the benefits of technology will be shared and experienced by all, rich and poor, powerful and powerless alike, and that our digital society will continue to be rated as good, right, and acceptable.

During the past two decades, we have experienced that the rapid progress of information technology in various forms has truly revolutionized the way we live, work, communicate, socialize, entertain, and protect ourselves and our own. This has brought many powerful benefits but also no small number of serious problems, challenges, and conflicts of interest, engendered by the enormous social and ethical implications of the new and largely unregulated world that we are creating.

Ethics are all about rights and wrongs, morals, principles, laws, and rules. Technology is about building tools that help us get things done more easily and efficiently. When we put the two together as "Technology Ethics," we are concerned with how to develop, build, and use technology in a way that enables us to accomplish our tasks, goals, and aspirations within the constraints of what is good, right, and acceptable to all stakeholders, without any unintended and unforeseen negative consequences.

Quantum Computing and AI

There are two natural applications of quantum computing that we can point out. The first application is to build classical machine learning and artificial intelligence algorithms that are better than classical algorithms. We can use quantum properties to bridge the gap between the likelihood of two distinct data distributions. The Hilbert space in which the quantum system can live is exponentially big and we cannot simulate it classically. This is the idea behind quantum algorithms for kernel support vector machines, where we look for a transformation of the input space so that a sphere in the transformed space models the linear decision boundary in the original space. The kernel can be simply expressed by looking at the inner products for every pair of samples and estimating their projection, but the estimation will actually be computed with the exponential of the dot product of the possibly non-linear embedding function of each sample. The old quantum algorithm for kernelized support vector machines follows a simple trick. They estimate the inner product of the pair of data using a quantum algorithm using a time running in the order of the square root of the estimation error. After the algorithm builds the (approximately) maximum eigenvalues of the kernel matrix, we can build the support vector machine. The quantum version of the kernel function is represented by performing the mapping to every pair of data points that belong to a feature of the quantum algorithm.

Quantum computing is a field that derives from the intersection of physics, complexity theory, and computer science. Current classical computers do not have the ability to simulate complex quantum systems because of the sheer vastness of states that a quantum system can have. For example, simulating only 42 electrons takes 1 petabyte of data. This fact has led to the development of novel quantum algorithms that try to take advantage of this ability of quantum computers to deal with a vast number of states. The true impact of quantum computing on artificial intelligence is not yet known. Some doubt its relevance, as it is highly specialized and may not turn around intelligent agents as easily as expected.